A Victims X Survivor's Diary Book of Poetry

Lisa Pearson

PAGE PUBLISHING, INC.
Conneaut Lake, PA

First originally published by Page Publishing 2020

ISBN 978-1-6624-3299-6 (pbk)
ISBN 978-1-6624-3300-9 (digital)

Printed in the United States of America

A SHEDDING

Kneeling, I sink my feeble knees
Into the spongy stretch of clay that is my brokenness.

Looking down at the vast marsh of despair; my
vision is sharpened by the chill of oppression.

An ending of myself—
I will inundate a downpour of tears;
drenching this already sodden soil
with the darkness that floods my being.

A body, a mind, a spirit
ravaged and violated by evil sins;
today will peal from its bones
the ominous mass of acclivities.

Standing, I print with the soles of my feet
the chaos and deformities that bound and proportioned
my raped, beaten and sodomized soul.

A life stormed by man's moral failures,
the most grievous damnations;
I'll shed with every strengthening step
of liberation.

BEASTS

Wounds flooded by the remnants of beasts. Like
the mating season of angry serpents—A slithering
entanglement of madness revisits the mind.
Coiled nightmares lay traps for the wakening of day. Scales
of barbed wire meant to keep scars from healing.
Shallow muddy waters thicken with every escaping step.
Heavy is the monstrous pits in which she sleeps.

DEAD GRASS

My afflicted heart lay beating
in the thirst of dead grass;
gold tones drinking spillage
laced with truths.

The rolling hills of this capricious field echo reticent
love sounds that gloss the air with hymns of agony.
Clearing skies reveal my wounds for rays
to fossilize creations damned.

A war leaving behind only a pale bereaving shadow…
and Here I thought a battle
was nothing new.

DEATH'S DOOR

Can you be torn when born…
A heart stopping
not one, not two, but three times.
Do we lose a piece of our soul when we
Wade the in-Between
I feel broke
Like I'm only pieces of a whole
I not only grazed the doors of death
I touched and twisted the frigid knob.
Released the colds stinging burn
I grabbed the winds of breath.
Most days I think…frozen shaved scales of my idle
touch imprinted deaths lasting latch. Eerily I believe I
have pieces of me calling to me…waiting on me…
As if to return what was stolen from me.

DESTRUCTION

It didn't begin on its own
Nudges leaving blackened contusions
Bumps without clemency.
Jolts of chaos bending bones.
A running punt of contention…
All started the trundling
of this bleeding stone.
Rolling with haste to save my soul.
Rolling cold like a shriek of thunder.
Rolling like grey angry skies
raging with captive gas-lit dew.
A flaming catapult released this
rocky beating mold.

FAITH

This pained heart,
he gifts, it beats…
beats to feed things unstitched.
Leaking veins seek to unleash;
weaved calligraphy to stain skins of demon's
hide to bind a survivor's spine.
There is a fire
he knows needs burned.
Edges that need scorch ;
a cover that must echo insidious screams.
I'll be concealed in ashes when I'm done;
having climbed from the darkest edge.
And he will be there as he always has;
in the frailty of my mind
twined tightly round the bars
that wall this aching chest.
cradling the weakest me,
rocking the strength in me.

HIDDEN GARDEN

Soil that began but a smirch, or so
was many seasons rumination.
Encroaching weeds; would be usurpers
with Intent to hinder flourishing.
Disarticulation is a prerequisite for could-be loam.
Yielding seasons bear the labor and suffering
of tribulations; bringing about attainment.
Now with much care and procurement
real development takes hold.
Something new beginning to mold—
Complete utter vicissitude.
This Garden, once seemingly sullied soot.
Now an effervescent thriving Novelty.
Such a shame the beauty beneath the dirt was
stomped down and overlooked; buried
by so much tedious hurt.

HOPELESS

No beatable heart fills this cavity.
It lays below the
Crushing encumbrance of life's murky depths.

Dying is no longer the formidable foe.
Ravenous trenches stole that reign…
Grasping rapaciously
Hopes ebbing immersion.

Drowning slowly
What death unquenchably craves.
Praying for hands
Is futile when their weight
Bears useless chest compressions.

STANDING GUARD

Her innocence resides
where all the monsters hide.

We become shackled to our demons in one way or another. Yes,
we move on through milestones. But the pieces claimed lurk
in the corridors of our minds. Not to hide but to make sure we
survive! Keeping at bay the residual entities hungry for our light.

KNOCK, KNOCK

Open the unhinged splintered doors.
There are windows…
Dusty windows need more than cracks
Where are you?
Do you need air?
Oh those houses…
So many musty nefarious houses.
Tell me; did the faucets run?
Rusted orange bleeding spouts.
Is your soul well?
A manifold of stones cast from evil, wicked hoarding bones.
Why are you still lurking soaked miles of tear filled walls?
Planks containing the saddest crying sounds…
Each walked memory a sharp untuned piano key.
You don't belong in there.
Listen to me—
You're merely bound by a past pain's suffering.
Your mind trapped in skins of scars and
bones of forever dented bruising.
All alone with fossilized ore.
Don't you see…those houses were not
Your home.
Chisel the thick lead paint holding the seals;
Use your withered tired hands to open what's been
stuck. Winds to carry away webs of torment
Blowing loose shedding of your life's upheaval.
Yes, it was all once so hauntingly real…
But, it's now your time to heal.

MY GOD—

Oh—
My Loving God—
hear me…

I have breathed in
—And—
Oh…My God—
how I have breathed out
the slow oxidized burning sting
that is life's stampeding pyre.

Trampled, bent, and crushed
are these brittle friable bones that
stay and lay idling wayside.

This pain won't relinquish its hold
Oh, how to my skin it clings.
My God—
A hurricane would be a kinder shelter
than the prison to which my soul is sewn.

MY PEN

Some days my heart is heavy with an
unexplainable sadness.
Heavy like a boulder being rolled up a rough terrain.
I walk heavily through my day, smiling
Every passing soul being none the wiser.
Some days it lasts as briefly as a slow traveling
gray storm cloud showering us to wash clean
the residue of our yesterday.
Other days it sticks to my chest walls pulling at my
strings—picking through my dusty wistful memories.
This addicted heart of mine likes its pain.
Yearning for bereavement to keep the
happiness paralyzed.
Languishing over her forever muse.
Oh how she prefers the weight of the doleful…
for it is the rock that imprints her ink.

MOTHERLESS

Drowning…
Have you ever nearly drowned?
Literally or Figuratively?
Both?
As a child, I fell from a boat. My mother watched as I was
literally drowning. She stayed in the safety of the boat.
As a child I fell through life.
My mother watched as I was figuratively drowning. A loved one
swam from shore to save me from my inability to swim the day
I fell from the boat. The fear felt that day is still eerily with me.
Watching as my mother watched and kept herself safely in the
boat was an inauspicious, most eerie feeling still with me. No
loved ones saved me as a child falling through life. I didn't have
to watch my mother watch me falling as she was the one holding
me under, pushing me down. I was forced to swim on my own.
No float, no life vest, no savior…
A mother should be a float; a mother should be
a life vest. A child with a mother shouldn't need
a savior. I wasn't a child with a mother.
Drowning…
Have you ever nearly drowned?
Literally or figuratively?
Both?
As a child I fell from a boat.

PTSD

Lingering ghosts trailing my heels.
Dedicated clinging shadows.
Today—Tomorrow—Yesterday
Always something new reflecting old.
Or is that just these shadows twisting my view?
These shadows, do they grow when the old creates new?
Or is it the new reshaping the old to become brand new?
Confusing, these ghostly shadows that are my deep obstinate roots.
My days—are they ever really new?
Or am I living a reissued time loop?

RECKONING

The day my reckoning began…
I heard the culling,
I felt and saw the signs.
A body fell frail,
by storms withering of decaying bones.

Life's noose turned these limbs cold;
this knotted beatless heart of mine
hushing all my cries.
No longer am I
bound or tethered
by strings of living hell.

Rupturing roots seeping of
malignant wreckage
Extend this reel of vitality
to the horizon…
Take me—Claim me.
Lay my gray flesh
into graveyard depths.

REGRETS

Rattle an ivory prison
We are full
Pick us clean
Fracture an opening to scrape loose the residing
residue of tolerated unsaid shit
A hoarding of dark rotted remnants
Move forward casting reaffirmations
Startling unheard Vocals strike a chord liberating locked truth.
A prison made even of bones can Unleash its festering beast
Don't just speak—
Scream…that's your key!

EXIT WOUNDS

A trigger; always cocked ready to fire your bullets.
Agonizing, to be forced to relive past pains;
choosing to remain your unflinching target.
Self-inflicted pain with no gain.
Reflections resembling hope insight my fight or flight response.
Yet I remained.
Burrowed inside me are pieces I'll never release; sewn in
fragments that reshaped my stubborn perceptions.
Those I'll hold tight.
I've realized the fight is over;
all that's left is flight.
My shield is up.
Your once loud trigger has lost its sound.
A silent explosion I no longer feel but at
last finally, vibrantly—I see.

SANDS OF TIME

Too much of being used
Like the bearers of ancient Egypt
Souls crushed under the weight of stone
Carried on shoulders. Building houses not lived in. Feet grinding
into the red sands of the desert. Worthy of more than the
lashings of the leather whips tearing through flesh. Shredding
spirits carelessly with endless thoughtlessness. Veins rupturing
from basking in the day's raging Sun. Burning eyes that
dare stare to the heavens. Lost in a stretch of
time. Theirs is theirs and mine is mine.
Thirst…an all-consuming thirst.
Silent screams that can't be heard
from the depths of ruins. If heard winds would carry songs of
hope that broken, worn bodies could sail To an everlasting river.
Weakened bones would be washed clean,
spirits revitalized. Instead, quietly they perished beneath the
rolling hills of stained sands where deep red blood was spilled.
Never tasting, feeling, or seeing what a place in
time refused. Lived and died used…

MY SCARS ARE MY ARMY

From infancy—
I struggled for breath.
I lost breath.
I regained breath.
I struggled for heartbeats.
I lost heartbeats.
I regained heartbeats.
That was just my beginning—the beginning of my scars.
From youth—
I struggled to live.
I lost sight of life.
I regained the will to live.
I struggled to survive.
I lost things, I thought I wouldn't survive.
I regained will to persevere.
That was the embedding—the embedding of my scars.
Each scar a weaponized splinter.
Each scar keener than your angled shattered pieces of glass.
Your glass may be designed to penetrate,
cut down, and wound.
My splintered scars are designed to stay firm, protect and shield
from insignificant, weak, fragile shards of ignorantly aimed glass.
My scars were forged from battles; they are splinters ready for war!
Your glass, though sharp; is delicately frangible,
leaving you with not even a shield.
One needs a Shield to face one's Army.

SHE, WHO'S BROKEN, HIDES

Joyful is the spirit.
Somber is the soul.
Half fell into darkness.
Half clambered to light.
I am not connected—unsewn—yet I am whole.
Two pieces of an oddity.
Wondering
Searching
A cascading trench under lock and key.
A time when innocence is fragile.
Trapped became she who needs me.
The piece that dominates my soul.
Have you ever peered at a placid pond and thought…
That's my soul.
A mirror reflecting how the ripples are gone.
They are with her.
She is waiting on serenity.
A safety net to grasp for climbing from shadows.
As I am the strength created from her suffering.
Oh how a yearning for happiness to vibrate my sensibilities as the
sorrows she is bound renders my soul from ever being found.

SILENT CANCERS

No one can save us from
the wicked...from the dark...
the unexplained ominous spasms
whispering repetitive crippling darkness
through twitching restless nerves.

Invisible serpents
coiling physical manifestations
that cut, bend, break, and bleed
our frozen souls into a shockwave
forever bound to an echo.

Corruption metastasized by
an invasion of sinister inhabitants
relentless in gnawing on aging bones.
These insanities whittle deep at our wills
charring edges to magnify only illusory light.

SIRENS

Deceiving meditation
Thrashing imaginations
Violently beautiful rumination
Brain spinning as if possessed by a fiend.
Scratching like an animal on the cell that is my fossilized
skull—my barrier to the remains of an insidious past. Screaming
restless sirens. Blood drips from a blade they use to repeatedly
slice my thoughts for endless servings of a velvet delicacy.
I taste each drop with my fingertips for savoring.

SKIN-DEEP

Her face reflects warmth through
radiant smiles. Her eyes reflect hurt
otherwise never seen.
She breathes as if drowning in waves
from the roughest seas.
She never speaks of the pain
carried skin-deep. Her walk glides on
grace, not learned easily.
Her presence is genuine
Love…as she gives freely what she
has never received. She survived
what sadly put to waste and drowned most.
She holds her beaten battered pieces
together so others believe in strength.
Her smile though…hiding all you'd
never otherwise know.

SURVIVING

Insidious thoughts called to the night
—or—was it me setting course
for the eventide.
In hopes of reaching black skies.
Eager Circling Vultures
Plucked a riddled conscious.
Madness ceased negotiations
Weakening this feeble carcass.
These roots wanted to bury deep
"Ashes further than six feet"
—They screamed—
—They screamed—
—They screamed—
Oh…how these roots screamed the most horrific curdling screams.
From fingertips to unhesitant lips
Down, down it goes
Silence falls
Lids close
Venin dreams I rode.
Till dawn's warmth woke that which I wished had frozen.

TEARDROPS

Unrelenting sparkling pearls of
pain that can only roll down as we rise
with our contradictory masks. Held back
like leftover droplets of rain
that settle into the crevices of a lonely withered
tree's brittle leaves; just waiting on a
gust of wind to set them free. The perfect
storm with the perfect breeze.
To shed them, scatter them, plant them, where
they'll forever leave fingerprints in time.
Only we will know of the thousand trickled seeds with so much
untold. What an unveiling to behold once we let them go.

BIRTHED BINDINGS

The Monsters that Built Me,
They have names.
Names I do not speak.
I won't dive too deep.
In the deep is where prey is kept.
—WAIT—LET ME Breathe—GO
Meet:
Pernicious-Vile-Nefarious-Baneful
—THESE MONSTERS BUILT ME!
They sought out to Destroy innocence.
That innocence now drives me.
I keep them collated.
Chapters to fill a book.
It will tell all they took.

THE PURGE

Strengthen our weary mind with the sanity
it so desperately yearns.
Let free this thudding thumping heart that's
been growing so damn weak.
—You request this, though life's long painfully
bleeding rivers of pleading weeps; I hear you
ask me, "Do I know the things that skulk,
lurk, and creep?" Oh, I do!
Oh—how I know what you've lived, what you've escaped,
what you relive in your screaming nightly dreams. Please
reach for me—I've got you now! You are my scared
innocent piece…please let go—it's killing me!
Imagine demons scurrying to the top of mountain peaks; reaching
for a slightly sun they'll never see. Blind beings keeping you
from seeing the peace you seek. Racing, clawing, scraping, and
tearing through the path I'm trying to take us through. They keep
digging valleys with their trampling stampede. Keeping scars fresh
to stay warm in the cozy depths they've dug for us—for you.
They've scattered our mental home bruising my aging bones.
I beg you Sweet girl, Purge our dusty tattered soul. Help
me evict what no longer has the power to dwell. Take my
hand—I need you if I'm going to escape the insane.

THE SOUNDS OF YOUR FEET

Oh darling,
how you've wandered off your path;
down thick bore of my corroded branches.

Enchanting charm
your mystic fog,
momentarily massaging leaves I bleed.

Familiar chills
crawling cold,
creeping like dew on mossy stones.

The deep dark of the wood,
unbeknownst to you…
the unwanted playground
of my soul's haunted home.

A wilderness
twisting crooked this spine
keeping aware
the twines of my mind.

When moonlight shines
you will see…
I'm more than a grove;
I am a bed of bedded trees
with roots to sense the most wicked feet.

THUNDER

There are dark clouds today,
roaring and rolling with triggered
hungry memories.
A storm's eye set on maiming
what's left of a soul it still craves.
Thunder explodes throughout the grisly clay
of the grey drenching charcoal that
claims this day.
Streams of lighting cracked like an endless whip
further than even dry eyes could see.
It's as if Zeus himself unleashed his fury
with a single vibrating mumble.
Releasing an unceasing symphony of cascading
torrents to drown any clinging vigor.
No shelter except this pale shivering skin.
It's only my bones
left holding on.
Holding on to this swirling debris,
that feeds the purgatory she sleeps, eats, and breathes.

UNDONE

Coming undone—onlookers' view
Something wrong.
Not thinking about an aftermath
Still Deep within me.
Punishment of what can't be seen
Nothing comes out right
While the world spins round, I'm no longer so tightly wound.
Eyes closed tight, just recklessly dancing in the bright
lights that fill what was once only darkened night.
Releasing every bit of wreckage that would
burden my open-eyed sight.
Blues radiating through every lively
motion as if in slow movement with the most
beautiful song I myself could have sung.
Is it wrong to let something wrong come so beautifully undone?

UNINVITED

Cage me!
No one can save me—
Oh, how I need saving!
Please cage me!
Cage me...after what's been stirring
Is no longer my beast!
Cage me...so my flesh is no longer crawled beneath.
Cage me, Please...
I don't want to escape!
That beast must never find its way
back underneath.

VITALITY

What looks so able is merely an orb of armor encasing
a delicate wilting red-black-laced rose.
She is fragility mirroring strength.
Like the way the slightest gust of wind grazing the decay of a resting
body with an open tomb could carry away the remaining form.
Her case is her blanket of security.
A mournful heart that hums its siren sounds so low that only a
tender ear caressed upon her aching chest bones could hear.
Her wounds are the brittle stem that barely holds
the drying petals of her weeping soul.
Her spirit though…
It will forever be the binding mold.

WRATH

A poisoned existence in frozen stasis now in the stages of life's decay.
Wanting to reach out your miserable
unloving hands to me.
Gurgling tears you falsely weep—
Clenching your throat, trying to breathe.
That'd be the bleeding rivers you
once choked, stomped, and beat out of me.
Your trembling, bent, weak knees will do no
good to kneel at my battered feet.
Exhausted from holding the weight of your
cruel, cold, harsh inabilities.
These shoulders you birthed traveled weary, wicked, lonely
roads carrying your buckets of oppressed cumbersome stones.
Tell me—Is it Forgiveness or selfish salvation you seek?
I'd ask that you spare me…
But as leeching monsters go—
The feast is never complete 'til it picks clean its stained
teeth, savors it s fleshy meat, swallowing whole it's
Preyed upon innocent souls.

WRECKAGE

Prude like a flower that never bloomed
They don't know the wreckage it holds
Curious like vultures
Ready to pick apart the sleeping beauty
Only baring seeds to those who would plant their own.
Meddlesome, intrusive, inquisitors need flapping feathers stung
A paralytic sting for seeking to only pluck away pulchritude.
Leaving but a stem.

ABOUT THE AUTHOR

 A woman misunderstood is the crown the author bears. Lisa Pearson is a devoted mother and a happily employed member of society. All the while she feels buried or underwater most of her days. As she is a woman of fathomless depth, the need to come up for air through the expression of sublime lit is forever pressing. That unleashing balance is how she walks the line of life's silver lining. Her childhood was that of neglect and abuses no child should endure. To this day, Lisa walks hand in hand with her past as it relentlessly aids in the writing she releases with every new chapter her life unfolds. While abuses created her, she has found that the inflictions which branded her also gifted her a unique ability to sew compassion and empathy within all her broken pieces. Attributes embodied that know no bounds, and for that, she holds a pen that freely vents the light beneath her suffering. She is merely pain's puzzling, refined creation.

CPSIA information can be obtained
at www.ICGtesting.com
Printed in the USA
BVHW072250021121
620543BV00004B/309